20 to 21

Abby Louise Cameron

BookLeaf Publishing

India | USA | UK

Presentation by *BookLeaf Publishing*

Web: www.bookleafpub.com

E-mail: info@bookleafpub.com

ISBN: 9789357446709

First edition 2022

DEDICATION

For 22

ACKNOWLEDGEMENT

A big thank you to BookLeaf Publishing for the very cool and weirdly timed opportunity.

Thank you to Vit Kannin for the beautiful cover art.

Thanks to the couple of people who kept this a secret.

And thanks to anyone who purchased a copy of this. You really didn't have to.

PREFACE

When I turned 20, I decided I wanted to write and collect a year of poems. Just for me, because I don't especially enjoy writing poems - really just not my jam. But I started to regularly write in my spare time, adding all the poems to a document called '20 to 21'. The title worked on two levels, because it's both the period of my life I was completing this in and 2021 is also the year that the majority of the series would be written in. But it was going to be just for me.

Coincidence said otherwise. I got an ad online saying that entries closed at midnight that night for a chance to publish a paperback of a few poems.

Specifically 21 poems. I figured that was a lucky number for the publishers to be offering; 21 poems written between the ages of 20 and 21.

Not just that - they all were due for final submission on the 21st of October, the exact 6 month mark between my two birthdays.

So I took all that as too cool a sign not to make use of, and did this. Partially because I thought it was pretty funny to unveil a published booklet of poetry, and partially because I thought this would be a cool keepsake from this time in my life. It was also a decent lockdown experiment to kill time.

Here are 21 poems written by a 20 year old, who now vaguely enjoys writing poetry a little more but still really doesn't like any of these. But they exist, and that's something.

Waiting Room

Golden years
Waltz with ghosts
Miss the known
Dream of mosts

Greener grass
To either side
Tired of waiting
Fear the tide

Gardens of Babylon
Litter your head
Name never called
Soon you'll be dead

Golden year patience
Wishing for then
Still hands are itching
Still asking 'when?'

Garden of Exxon

Net below factory windows
Black film across the waves
Bury the backlash they'll all soon know
Never ask what might've been saved

Wonder now if it's far too late
Any purity slowly dilutes
Abandon now thy ship of state
Though no crew member bit the fruit

Stone fruit of gain
Worth heavenly exile
Loop that refrain
In the dregs of your Nile

Reset a compass towards any Messiah
Can't believe barrels would come from a liar

Halley's Comet

Time it right
To catch her twice
But well beyond the reach of men
If we say goodbye
If you ever die
Halley's comet will come again
We wanted too much
Burned all that we touched
But this the wealthy can't share
I'll hold you close
I'll miss you most
But Halley's happy in the air
After us
After loss
After everything I hold dear
Trust in this
Above our tryst
Halley's comet will appear

Venus

Somewhere in some distant sky
Straight till morning and a bit to the right
They used toothpicks and scraped every corner
Emptied her out but no one could mourn her
Fool us once, ignorant bliss melts ice
But the blame's on us, it happened twice
The backlash won't always feel like a dream
Heaven accept a sorry just from me
What children trampled you down to bones
Are you happier up there and all alone?
Love watch down as we do it again
Drink paper straws, helpless one step for men
Give us a garden to start all anew
No doubt we'll spill oil down that coastline too
A bottle still floats long after we've left
Solitude's a gift for all the rest

Sounds Like a Prayer

Sing a lullaby
Ease a small child to sleep
Blend your breaths on your chest
Rub their back, stop their weep
Humming words you've forgotten
But you know the love and care
It feels like forever
It sounds like a prayer

Try to keep eyes open
Barred television glow
Waiting for the world to end
Waiting for something to know
Vending machine hums
Through cool and sterile air
It tastes like mid-flight dinner
It sounds like a prayer

Cackling on the weekend
But still there come every Tuesday
You lose the cynicism

Forget the things you used to say
When his head throws back in laughter
Nothing's ever felt so rare
As his name escapes your lips
It sounds like a prayer

Rolling waves against a boat
Awake and shoulder to shoulder
Wishing some sense for what you've seen
Wishing you were bolder
Jealousy isn't in you
For those who've found a peace unshared
It's heavy breaths and dreaming
It sounds like a prayer

Stand in a crowd of thousands
But these words are only yours
Fingers stretch up to the heavens
Feel that bass thrum in awe
A chorus of voices
Know this love as only theirs
It's a song you'll likely skip one day
It sounds like a prayer

Crowded streets and begging bowls
Keeping eyes averted
Know your blessings are just luck pure
Wondering if you've earned it
The bustle of commuters

Drowns out cries for something fair
It's a cacophony of hunger
It sounds like a prayer

Silent cathedral somewhere foreign
Pause the earpiece tour guide
Stained glass and unreachable art
A thoughtlessness you can't confide
Do we make magnificent things anymore?
Does a Father miss the flair?
Light a candle in eery quiet
It sounds like a prayer

Unsure words; you'll be okay
Reuniting terminal squeal
Whispers when you'd better sleep
The way a cello makes you feel
A rib aching laugh
First wail meets first air
Midnight final breath unheard
It sounds just like a prayer

1/12

All of October
A tiny screen
Watching self portraits
Unplugging your dreams

Black out a month
A whole world at your nails
Time's an avalanche
All is to no avail

We Were Here

Make the painful call
Try and seek the truths
But choose despite the fossils
Head over heels over blues
Break your heart and heal it over
No message after the tone
If you really want to be special
You choose to be alone
Think you can unravel
What never has been clear
Carve into the walls of a cave
'I, too, was here'

From the Fridge

Penny drop
Unlit fuse
Your mess to mop
Just a muse
Silent musing from the chill
2-dimension NPC
To inspire falls and thrills
Was no more to ever be
Disappeared to push you on
Suffering to service
Manic pixie dreaming con
Story held from surface
Mourning touchable velvet frock
Needs nothing done to please her
Please feel free to ignore the knock
From the woman in your freezer

For Her

A drop for Ophelia
Another for Juliet
A glass for Eurydice
And the sun she'll never get
A toast for boy bands
And things made for you
A drop for the past
And one for me too

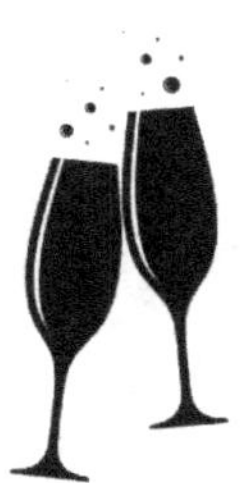

Fortune Teller

Sun and moon rising
Live and die for nothing guaranteed
A meaning so enticing
Beg the fortune teller for any heed
Find her in the blue light
Sole survivor with a flare
Willing to let anyone enlight
The carnival booth must care
Can't find her in art
Or in some spirit trend
Someone tell us where to start
So we can stop thinking about the end

20 to 21

We're two decades down
Apparently everything is limited
Sound of a heart, a ticking clock
A fear that feels so primitive

Defence for trial by a prewritten Lord
Either way you'll go down as not quite done
No one gets to finish the chord
You'll be left with song unsung

Holding ticks like water in my hands
Another night of eyes on ceilings
Asking how you do the most with what you've
got
And what to do with drowning feelings

Through you another's notes endure
The hum they never finished
Carry the tune and make others sing yours
Everything else will soon diminish

What's left might be heartbreak or lonely fun
Chase an audience, chase an impact
Try to make friends with twenty one
Or carve a mark and ignore the facts

Out with a whimper and a dusty cloud
Wishing you'd never landed
But that isn't allowed

Sirius (9 Canis Major)

A star topples down from a handmade sky
And shards shatter down upon idyllic views
The same omnipotent hand that hung every light
Will cue the sun and pass on the news
The cameraman calls everything mine
Turn the sponsored bottle to fill the screen
The sort of thing you read by Naomi Klein
Find some kind of solace in logoless jeans
Sail toward a space without commercials or eyes
Wonder why we love to be on display
Ignore what the radio justifies
Be glad you were there when the sky fell that
day

Take your final bow on the pale blue step
Something else awaits, just don't know what yet

Type 4

Obsession with the ingenue
1 in billions but wholly new
Holding on to films too tight
Not because no one else can be right
But for the stomach churning fear
That everyone feels what you hold dear

Scroll back through assignment feedback
To find the memorised praise well tracked
Assurance of special, in some way
A jealousy of everyone every day
And yet the hypocrisy
To think they can't see what you see
Count the ENFPs who need a stage
Insist you should live on through the page
Despise with every fibre of your being
Try to blacken the great big future you're seeing

Crocodile Ticks

Hundred and seven billionth to feel it
Leave the nocturnal fearing behind
Can't swim with it there as it tugs below waves
Shed it before thirty if you plan to survive
Hooked on the promise of something great
You'll lose all five fingers and leave art unmade
Longing to freeze the metronome's threat
And everything else that Wendy forbade
Nails claw a cliff of unspent potential
Days never used to fall so torrential
Twenty and terrified to earn your one
You were always so scared of the buried drums
Fighting the tide is a bitter mock
The crocodile creeps with a tick and a tock

Class of 2007

Please look me in the eye
Lend anyone a hand
And look me in the eye
Pass me and let rules disband
I'll look you in the eye
I don't know what I'll do if you won't
Maybe when I catch your eye
Spirit can finally meet bone

Death of a Customer

Dreams will not be culled
Branded fingers round your throat still shine
Kitchen sink stories are suddenly dull
Prayer's a tin of morphine down the mine
Written in cards you never dealt
Find content within a dime a dozen
Someone has to care for things that melt
Treat obscurity like your own brand of rosin
Give up on escaping to farfetched pipes
The way things are sees all of it rigged
One day you'll realise you're still unripe
And that people who deal are rarely tricked

Let your buying in wane with an unhappy flicker
What monuments you'll build are only of wicker

Catch Up

After dramatising unsaid goodbyes
We caught up last night
For the sake of old times
Whole group dropped a hundred bombs
Not to know these things just felt so wrong
The awkward air of things yet unshared
But here we are and we all still care
Reminiscing about adolescent games
Starting all our stories with foreign names
The relief you messaged wanting to meet
To click your name was such a feat
Sickening knowledge that it felt so strange
Saw the middle momentum of unstopping
change

Gaia

Soaking up the rays from a mama
Thinking about some teenage drama
Wanting more than anyone can give

Fantasise about a daughter
Giving her the world and all its water
Learn how to let go and how to forgive

Pray she has a world to blame
Hope she hates the definition of fame
But despises the ingenue

Think about a motherly-daughterly love
Turn her eyes to a blinding above
But love her in the salty blue

Molasses

Lose another month to backlit fray
View the world like a thousand Monets
Wonder if the mirror's passé
Can't scrub molasses off your hands

To pen it is nothing
You have to do something
Before molasses seeps into your glands

Feel the blackhole when you're stuck in a room
How blue lights suddenly don't feel true
Molasses always seems to outrun
'Nowadays' likely has only begun
Eye straining headaches are solely on you

(Reprise)

Stuck at a fork in the road
Wondering when to let go of dreams
When the clown lets go of a helium load
There will be no reprise

Desperate for your initials to scratch
Splinters from a breaking bark
Against the clock you've met your match
Send on a kite your golden mark

In your hands are things unspent
A calling world and daunting spoils
What if there's no day for repent?
What if nothing becomes of toils?

Bright crimson nose
Stare at your painted eyes
Doesn't matter what role you chose
You never will reprise

Maybe it doesn't need to be terror
Find solace in a one-time shot
Stop trying so very hard to be clever
A couple seconds might be all you've got

Everything you make could always be gauche
Expecting the grand is not for this age
You choose each day to make 'failing' morose
Never can hear when the exit music plays

The 11 o'clock number cues right here
Are you going to chase the phantom thread?
Creation bliss may soothe the fears
Could mute the ticks as you rest your head

This, right now, must be enough
Maybe nothing more will come
No fruit born of what you love
Spend days like this, your will be done

Be someone who sees over someone who
clamours
For an out of reach wanting to be seen
With the streets and the now you must be
enamoured
Hope you won't care how memorable you've
been

Just one go - known that from the start
Relief replaces the anchor's sink
These things don't have to grip your heart
Is it enough to drench your days in ink?

You're petrified of what you might waste
Terrified to choose an ending rhyme
Stop thinking of things you might not taste
It's a blessing to choose how to spend your time

Don't worry about a final, lasting word
Remember how it felt to see the absurd

Curtain Call

Grew up like a trickling creek
Blinked and everything's out of reach
Push the curtain up to stop the call
But still pours down the waterfall
Take a bow and hope you've managed
I'll undo every shall I've damaged
Buy more time it make it right
Promise tomorrow I'll find the light
Try real hard to take nothing for granted
Try to accept that I never truly manned it
Spring will always suddenly come
But still the year is not yet done

www.ingramcontent.com/pod-product-compliance
Lightning Source LLC
Chambersburg PA
CBHW070615160726
48003CB00005B/2285